Amazon Kindle Fire HD 8 & 10 User Guide

The complete Kindle Fire HD Manual to Master Your New Kindle Fire Tablet

Rodney Barrett

ii

Copyright 2018 by Rodney Barrett - All rights reserved

The following book is reproduced with the goal of providing information that is as accurate and reliable as possible. Regardless, purchasing this book can be seen as consent to the fact that both the publisher and the author of this book are in no way experts on the topics discussed within and that any recommendations or suggestions that are made herein are for entertainment purposes only. Professionals should be consulted as needed prior to undertaking any of the action endorsed herein.

This declaration is deemed fair and valid by both the American Bar Association and the Committee of Publishers Association and is legally binding throughout the United States.

Furthermore, the transmission, duplication or reproduction of any of the following work including specific information will be considered an illegal act irrespective of if it is done electronically or in print. This extends to creating a secondary or tertiary copy of the work or a recorded copy and is only allowed with express written consent from the Publisher. All additional rights reserved.

The information in the following pages is broadly considered to be a truthful and accurate account of facts and as such any inattention, use or misuse of the information in question by the reader will render any resulting actions solely under their purview. There are no scenarios in which the publisher or the original author of this work can be in any fashion deemed liable for any hardship or damages that may befall them after undertaking information described herein.

Additionally, the information in the following pages is intended only for informational purposes and should thus be thought of as universal. As befitting its nature, it is presented without assurance regarding its prolonged validity or interim quality. Trademarks that are mentioned are done without written consent and can in no way be considered an endorsement from the trademark holder.

vi

TABLE OF CONTENTS

INTRODUCTION 1

CHAPTER 1: GETTING TO KNOW YOUR KINDLE FIRE HD 8 AND 10 5

How to Charge Your Kindle Fire......................... 5

How to Check If Your Device Is Charging.......... 8

How to Turn On Your Kindle Fire 12

Time to Register and Install Your Settings...... 14

How to Navigate on Your Kindle Fire.............. 28

Changing Your Kindle Fire HD Wallpaper 33

How to Use Your Quick Actions Panel to Change Your Kindle Fire Home Screen Wallpaper.. 35

How to Use the Bluetooth Pairing Feature on Your Kindle Fire... 36

Setting Up Your Email on Your Kindle Fire 40

How to Add a Second Email Account to Your Kindle Fire 46

Receiving Your Email Notifications on Your Kindle Fire 47

Setting a Timer for Emails on Your Kindle Fire49

Downloading Apps and Games on Your Kindle Fire 50

Downloading Videos on Your Kindle Fire 51

Uninstalling a App from Your Kindle Fire 52

Features Everyone Can Use 55

How to Add Secondary Keys to Your Keyboard 58

Why Do You Need Honey pot on Your Kindle Fire? 59

You Can Have a Multi-Screen to Multi-Task... 60

CHAPTER 2: HOW TO SHOP AND FIND ENTERTAINMENT ON YOUR HD FIRE 65

viii

Buying and Reading Books, Magazines, and Periodicals on Your Kindle Fire 65

Downloading Free Books to Your Kindle Fire . 68

Removing a Book from Your Kindle Fire 69

Transferring Files to Your Kindle Fire 71

Downloading YouTube app on Your Kindle Fire 73

Downloading YouTube Videos on Your Kindle Fire 80

Downloading Music on Your Kindle Fire 86

Downloading Audiobooks on Your Kindle Fire 92

Bluetooth Pairing of a Speaker to Your Kindle Fire 96

Mirroring Your Kindle Fire Screen to Your TV 98

Taking Pictures with the Camera on Your Kindle Fire 100

CHAPTER 3: WHAT REALLY IS ALEXA? 103

Enabling Alexa on Your Kindle Fire 107

Some Do's and Don'ts with Alexa 108

Activating Hands-Free Mode........................ 110

How to Use Alexa to Listen Audios on Your
Kindle Fire.. 111

How to Use Alexa with Audiobooks on Your
Kindle Fire.. 115

Commands to Use with Alexa for Books: 118

CHAPTER 4: TROUBLESHOOTING AND COMMON ISSUES OF THE KINDLE FIRE 121

Not Connecting To Wi-Fi 121

Flickering Issues with Your Kindle Fire Screen
.... 123

Crashing or Freezing of the Silk Browser...... 125

When Your Kindle Fire Is Not Charging 125

What to Do when the MicroSD Card Is Not
Recognized or Does Not Work 127

Erratic Keyboard Typing 129

CONCLUSION 133

CHECK OUT OTHER BOOKS 135

Introduction

I love technology. New devices excite me and I just want to be left alone to discover the hidden features of my new technological gadget.

When I unravel hidden features on a new device, I get that butterfly feeling in my stomach.

Yes, I know that not everyone shares my love for technology and some people struggle with just finding the power button on a device.

That is why I want to help those who either are struggling with finding the power button on a gadget or those who are pros like me to unravel the magnificent features of one of the best devices on the market right now.

Amazon is the mega online shopping platform that aims to always increase the satisfaction of its customers. Thus, it should not be surprising that its latest generation of Kindle Fire has been the buzz topic among technology lovers.

Among the remarkable features of the latest generation of Kindle Fire is Alexa!

Oh, my! You have no idea what Alexa can do? Well, saddle up, stretch your fingers and start clicking your way through my guide.

Introduction

My guide is feature-information packed that is guaranteed to amaze you just as how Amazon's latest generation of Kindle Fire is super amazing.

Hey, are you ready for your foot-shaking toe-curling technology experience? Yes, it will be that exciting. Come take a read! My guide is a reader's fun-filled information adventure about the Kindle Fire HD 8 and 10.

4

Chapter 1: Getting To Know Your Kindle Fire HD 8 And 10

How to Charge Your Kindle Fire

I am yet to purchase a technological device that does not require charging. Therefore, I know that the Kindle Fire HD 8 or 10 gadgets will also require charging.

Yeah, you are quite right! It can be a spoiler of the moment especially when excitement is tickling your every fiber to find those mysterious features to brag to your friends and family about what your device can do.

Amazon Kindle Fire HD 8 & 10 User Guide

Let us not waste any more time talking about it. I will now tell you how to charge your new tech-baby to get it all powered up for your feature adventure.

So, there are two channels to get your device charged and anyone of the channels can be used to charge your Kindle Fire HD 8 or 10. One of them; however, will get the job done in less time than the other. But I will tell you about both methods and you can then choose which one suit you best.

The longer method is by using the USB cable. You would insert the larger end of the cable into your computer or laptop and the smaller end into your Kindle Fire HD. *If you are going to use your computer or laptop to charge your Kindle Fire HD, please ensure that the computer*

Chapter 1: Getting To Know Your Kindle Fire HD 8 & 10

or laptop is fully charged. Of course you will have to turn on your computer or laptop to use it to charge the Kindle Fire.

Right, I need to tell you where to find the USB cable slot on your Kindle Fire HD. My bad, please forgive.

Well, for the Kindle Fire HD 8 the USB cable slot is located between the power button and the slot for the headphone to the top of your device.

If you have the Kindle Fire HD 10, then, just look to the right of the device between the headphone slot and the device power button to find the USB cable slot.

Amazon Kindle Fire HD 8 & 10 User Guide

If you are for faster charging and more time discovering features, then, you definitely want to use your adaptor to charge up your tech-baby.

Using the adaptor to charge your device is a one-two step. Simply insert the smaller end of the adaptor into your Kindle Fire HD 8 or 10 (the same slot that you had inserted the smaller end of the USB cable into) then, the larger end into the adaptor and plug the adaptor into an electrical socket.

Bravo! Your device should be charging now.

How to Check If Your Device Is Charging

A glitch that sometimes pops its ugly head with various devices is that you will connect the

Chapter 1: Getting To Know Your Kindle Fire HD 8 & 10

necessary charging equipment to your device but unfortunately it does not charge. You want to ensure that this is not the case with your Kindle Fire. Therefore, before your mind wonders off to adventure land thinking about all the cool things, you will do with your Kindle Fire; please stop and check if it is actually charging first.

A lightning bolt normally appears on the Kindle Fire battery icon once the device is being charged. You can find your Kindle Fire battery icon to the top your device screen. You will also need to look to the bottom of your Kindle Fire screen for the indicator light which customarily has an amber color to demonstrate that it is charging.

Amazon Kindle Fire HD 8 & 10 User Guide

If any of the aforementioned charging signs does not appear, you will need to check if whatever you are using to charge your Kindle Fire is connected correctly to the device and to the source of electrical power.

If you have checked and everything is connected correctly and you are still not seeing the charging signals, then, try using a different charger with your Kindle Fire. Or you might also try whatever charger you are using with another device. If you use a different charger on your Kindle Fire and it works, then, the charger that came with your device is defected.

If you use a different charger on your Kindle Fire that is working properly and you also discover that the charger that came with the Kindle Fire is working, then, you will need to

10

Chapter 1: Getting To Know Your Kindle Fire HD 8 & 10

contact Amazon to inform them of the problem with your Kindle Fire. It is quite possible that they will replace your Kindle Fire if it is defected.

Okie dokie that gloom is out of the way; I do not like to speak of the glooms that come with technology. But I have to let you be informed of the options you have that you can have a great experience with your device.

So, it could be the case that you never had a charging problem with your Kindle Fire just as I never had one and so after approximately four hours your Kindle Fire should be fully charged if you had used the adaptor.

Amazon Kindle Fire HD 8 & 10 User Guide

To know when your Kindle Fire charged is a 100% complete the indicator light at the bottom will change from amber to green.

Great! You got a green light. Now it is time to unplug power up your tech-baby.

How to Turn On Your Kindle Fire

Remember early I told you how to locate your power button. If you have forgotten where it is located let me just give you a quick reminder to prevent you have to be going back to that page.

If you have the Kindle Fire HD 8, then, the power button is located at the top of your device.

Chapter 1: Getting To Know Your Kindle Fire HD 8 & 10

For the Kindle Fire HD 10 the power button is located to the right of your device.

Woo hoo! You have found your power button. Now all you need to do is to use one of your fingers – I like to use my index finger – to press on the power button for approximately 10 seconds or just count to about three and then release your finger.

Excellent! You are a fast learner my reader.

Oh a downer! You thought you would be able to use your Kindle Fire as soon as it finished booting up. Unfortunately, no you will have to register your device on Amazon and install a few settings. But, hey, it is no biggie. Amazon has made the steps very easy to follow and with the aid of my guide which is written to read like my voice is in your head, you will have things up and running in no time.

Let's keep the ball rolling. Stick with my guide and you will be astounded at the awesome features you will be able to install.

Time to Register and Install Your Settings

First thing your eyes will behold on your screen after it is booted up is a "Welcome Message" which I think is a nice gesture by Amazon developers.

It is time to move along to the other steps though.

Step 1: Language is important because that is how you will understand the process and

Chapter 1: Getting To Know Your Kindle Fire HD 8 & 10

whatever messages that will appear on your Kindle Fire. Therefore, it is time to select your preferred language for your Kindle Fire. You can select your preferred language by looking at the top of your Kindle Fire home screen to the left for the option.

If you would like to enlarge the size of the text for your Kindle Fire the option to do Is at the bottom of your device home screen. Look for the tab with the words "**Text Size**" and select your preferred text size.

Your Kindle Fire language is set and your text size is also to your preference. It is now time to tap on the option "**Continue**" that is at the bottom to the right of your Kindle Fire screen.

Amazon Kindle Fire HD 8 & 10 User Guide

Step 2: Connecting to the world wide net is how you will be able to access a lot the fun features that you need. So let us get your Kindle Fire connected to your "**Wi-Fi Network**."

There will be a list of different networks choose the one that is your internet provider. It is a requirement that you enter the password for your "**Wi-Fi**" after you have selected your internet provided. Simply enter your password for your Wi-Fi network in the provided field. After entering your Wi-Fi password you then tap on the option to "**Connect.**" Waiting period for connection is dependent on the speed of our network.

Immediately after being connected to your Wi-Fi a message will appear prompting you to update the software on your Kindle Fire. There

Chapter 1: Getting To Know Your Kindle Fire HD 8 & 10

is no need to be alarmed when this message appears. Just go ahead and do the update. Again the completion of the update is dependent on the speed of your network.

Once the update is completed your Kindle Fire will do an automatic reboot.

Step 3: If you cannot remember your Amazon account login information and you have to write into your diary, then, it is time to go get that book because you need to login your Amazon account for this step.

*If you do not have an Amazon account, then, take a few seconds to get one by tapping on the option that says "**New To Amazon start here**."*

Amazon Kindle Fire HD 8 & 10 User Guide

There is one simple reason that you must login your Amazon account and that is because it is the only way the Kindle Fire HD 8 or 10 can become registered for you to have access to Amazon numerous benefits. Take for example you would like to use the Kindle Unlimited readers' benefit. If your Kindle Fire is not registered on Amazon, you will not be able to access that benefit.

So whether you have to grab your journal for your login information or you have to create an account go ahead and take few seconds to get it done.

However, if you are a little on the stubborn side - like I am – and you are adamant that you just want to see the home screen of your Kindle Fire; you can opt to tap on the option

Chapter 1: Getting To Know Your Kindle Fire HD 8 & 10

"**Complete Setup Later**." That will let you bypass the setting up process. But Amazon has a pop-up message installed that will prompt you about all the features that you will not be able to access if you do not complete the setup process. If that stubborn thought will not leave your mind and all you want to do is to go to your device home screen, then, you can tap on the option "**Skip**" which will take you to the next step.

If after you click on the tab "**Skip**" you somehow decide to ditch that stubborn thought after all, you can always tap on the option "**Cancel**" which will navigate you back to where you can complete the setup process.

I figure you must know that I will be taking the long route to tell you how to complete the registration process. After all, this would not be a complete guide if I do not tell you how to finish the registration of your device.

Step 4: So, tap, tap with your fingers and type in your login information for Amazon.

First thing that is required of you in this step is for you to check your "**Time Zone**" once your Kindle Fire is up to the time, then, all you have to do is look to the bottom right of the device screen for the tab with the word "**Continue**" and click on it.

Here is one of the first amazing things about your Kindle Fire HD, if you had previously owned one of Amazon Kindles and for whatever reason you might no longer have that device, you can now restore information from

Chapter 1: Getting To Know Your Kindle Fire HD 8 & 10

that device which was stored in Amazon cloud on your new Kindle Fire HD.

That's pretty amazing, right?

If you would like to restore information from a previous device, then, just go ahead and click on the tab "**Restore Your Fire.**"

If you never owned a Kindle Fire before or you are not interested to restore information from a previous device, then, the tab "**Do Not Restore**" would be the one you need to select now.

Step 5: *Okay, I can hardly restrain the excitement that is brewing inside of me for you! Seriously, we are nearing the point when you will be able to get to your home screen.*

Amazon Kindle Fire HD 8 & 10 User Guide

In this step you will get to activate benefits that you can share with your family members. That is why the option "**Family Setup**" is displaying.

The "**Amazon Free Time Unlimited**" benefit will give you the opportunity to download a maximum of 10,000 children friendly books. In fact it is not only books that you can download with the benefit but you will also be able to share apps and videos that you had purchased with the children that are added to the child's profile under your family setup. With the "**Free Time Unlimited**" you can add four children the child's profile settings.

Of course since the benefit is about family you will be able to add adults to your account too.

Chapter 1: Getting To Know Your Kindle Fire HD 8 & 10

You probably will need some time to think about whom you would like to add to your account under the family settings; therefore, you can just click on the tab with the words "**Not Now**" then, "**Continue**" at the bottom right of your screen to move to the next step.

Step 6: If you like your location to be known, then, you can enable the location service at this step. But, I must inform you that doing so is one of the medium by which your battery will easily use up. It is best to prevent from having apps running that will easily drain your battery. If you are like me and want to have less battery drainer apps and services, then, you would click on the tab "**No Thanks.**" If you want the location service you can also choose to enable it on your Kindle Fire.

Amazon Kindle Fire HD 8 & 10 User Guide

Step 7: Trust me when I tell you that this is a must enabler step. Without backup and auto-save on any technological device you are in for big trouble if your device has a sudden rebooting or shut down. Therefore, you should not hesitate to click on the tab to enable "**Backup & Auto-Save.**"

To how this feature is important Amazon normally has it automatically selected on Kindle Fires. That is how you will be able to restore information that is stored on Amazon cloud when you purchase a new Kindle Fire.

Even though Amazon tends to automatically enable the "**Backup & Auto-Save**" just take a few seconds to do a quick check and ensure there are no unselected options under this feature. After you have completed your

Chapter 1: Getting To Know Your Kindle Fire HD 8 & 10

checking, then, click on the tab "**Continue**" that is located at the bottom of your device screen.

Step 8: *In this day and age if there is a technological device that cannot connect to social media you can safely state it is defected. Social media is hub of professional and social connections around the globe.*

Fortunately for you, your Kindle Fire is **not defected** so you are now at the step that you can enable your favorite social media networks. To enable your favorite social networks tap on the option "**Connect Social Networks.**"

I am going to skip this option because we all have different social media networks and since I do not know which one is your favorite, I

Amazon Kindle Fire HD 8 & 10 User Guide

opted to tap on "**Continue**" at the bottom of screen.

Step 9: *Think of this stage as your better to be safe and protected than to be sorry.*

That statement might be a puzzle to you, so, I will explain what I mean. Amazon offers insurance coverage for your Kindle Fire.

With the Amazon insurance coverage for your Kindle Fire it is for two years and provides coverage for certain accidental damages. The price for the insurance is quite reasonable too.

Nevertheless, this is another benefit I opted to bypass since I do not know your financial situation. If you would like to bypass this

Chapter 1: Getting To Know Your Kindle Fire HD 8 & 10

benefit too, then, tab on the option "**No thanks**" to move to the next step.

Step 10: *If you would like to buckle-up your confidence level to navigate through the different features of your Kindle Fire this step can assist.*

Amazon has a list of tutorials built-in your Kindle Fire that you can scroll through. To move through the slides all you have to do is keep tapping on the option "**Next.**"

If you believe your confidence does not need a booster, then, just tap on the option "**Exit**" to end the tutorials.

Amazon Kindle Fire HD 8 & 10 User Guide

Hurray! You are now at your home screen. Your settings are activated and your device is registered on Amazon woo hoo!

How to Navigate on Your Kindle Fire

Observe the three figures on the above image carefully because they are your main navigation keys on your Kindle Fire HD.

You will find them at the bottom of the Kindle Fire home screen.

The "**Square**" tab is used to navigate to your "**Recent Apps**."

Sometimes we might use an app and forget to close it that it is not running in the background on our device. If this happens when you are

Chapter 1: Getting To Know Your Kindle Fire HD 8 & 10

using your Kindle Fire, then, you can use the "**Square**" tab to locate any of the recently used apps that are open in the background on your device.

It is useful to know how to locate your "**Recent Apps**" because when they are allowed to keep running in the background of your device they drain the battery.

If you do not know how to close a app that is running in the background of your Kindle Fire all you need to do is use the "**Recent Apps**" tab to find them and you use your finger to swipe from right to left to close any of the apps.

Located between the square and the triangle tabs is the "**Circle**" button which is the known as the "**Home Button**."

A tap on the "**Circle**" tab will take you to your home screen when you are using any app on your Kindle Fire.

Finally you have the "**Triangle**" tab which is called the "**Back button**."

How the "**Back button**" operates is that if you are browsing the internet for example, then, you happen to tap on link and then you realized that it is not the information you are searching for. You just tap on the "**Back button**" to navigate the previous page that you were on.

You can also use the "**Back button**" to navigate to your home screen. Sometimes it might take a couple taps to get to the home screen depending on the number places you navigated

Chapter 1: Getting To Know Your Kindle Fire HD 8 & 10

to from the last time you viewed your home screen.

Important: It is possible that you will not always see the navigation buttons being displayed at the bottom of your device screen. This mostly occurs when you might be viewing videos on the Kindle Fire. Once you are viewing a video and you want to use the navigation buttons, use your finger to swipe from the bottom of your Kindle Fire screen in an upwards direction and the tabs will appear.

Navigating Your Kindle Fire Using Shortcuts

We all have a bit of lazy streak within us so we want to know we have the door open for an easier option to doing things especially when we are dealing with technology.

Amazon Kindle Fire HD 8 & 10 User Guide

Well, your new tech-baby does have prebuilt shortcuts for navigation and we will now look at a few of them that you might find handy.

Now is a good time as every to practice using your "**Home Button.**" Tap on the home button to go to your home screen. Look to the top of your device there will be a list of tabs. For example you should be seeing *recent, home, books, vids, games* among the tabs listed at the top of your Kindle Fire home screen.

Based on the name of the tab that is listed on your home screen, you can use it to access apps or services pertaining to the name. Take for example the tab "**Books**" by clicking on that option it will take you to where your books are stored on your Kindle Fire.

Chapter 1: Getting To Know Your Kindle Fire HD 8 & 10

Not all the apps can be displayed directly on the your Kindle Fire home screen so to view the rest of apps use your finger to swipe from right to left and vice versa.

Important: The tab with the words "Silk Browser" it what you will need to click on to large an internet browser when you want to surf the net.

Changing Your Kindle Fire HD Wallpaper

I just love when I can let you use a feature that I told you about before – great practice session, right?

Step 1: Tap on your "**Home button,**" then, scroll and look for your "**Settings**" tab.

Step 2: Click on the "**Settings**" tab, then, select "**Display.**"

Step 3: Under the tab "**Display**" you will need to tap on the option "**Select Home Screen Wallpaper**."

You can truly personalize your Kindle Fire home screen wallpaper by clicking on the tab "**Your Photo**" and choose an image from your personal photo stash. *You could use your Kindle Fire to take a picture of yourself or transfer a picture for your cellular phone to your Kindle Fire. I will teach later how to transfer items to your Kindle Fire.*

The second option to change your home screen wallpaper is to select a photo from the prebuilt images that are on your Kindle Fire.

Chapter 1: Getting To Know Your Kindle Fire HD 8 & 10

How to Use Your Quick Actions Panel to Change Your Kindle Fire Home Screen Wallpaper

Yay! You get to use your navigation tabs again.

Step 1: You can either use the "**Home button**" or the "**Back button**" to go to your device home screen.

Step 2: To find your Kindle Fire "**Quick Actions Panel**" place your finger at the top of your home screen and swipe downwards.

Step 3: Scroll down to find the option "**Settings**" and select it.

Step 4: Click on the tab "**Display**" and then select "**Select Home Screen Wallpaper**."*You*

35

Amazon Kindle Fire HD 8 & 10 User Guide

can now follow the above-mentioned step to change the image on your Kindle Fire home screen

How to Use the Bluetooth Pairing Feature on Your Kindle Fire

It is worth mentioning that even though the Kindle Fire has the Bluetooth pairing feature it will not be able to pair with every accessory or device. *It is not unusual for devices Bluetooth pairing feature to not be compatible with every accessory or other devices.*

You can rest assured though that your Kindle Fire will be able to pair with some very useful wireless accessories that have the Bluetooth pairing feature. Two of the wireless accessories that can be paired with your Kindle Fire are:

Chapter 1: Getting To Know Your Kindle Fire HD 8 & 10

A keyboard — you might experience difficulty using the prebuilt keyboard on your Kindle Fire because you are accustomed to using larger keyboards. To fix that discomfort you can purchase a wireless keyboard that can be paired with your Kindle Fire.

A speaker — depending on your preferred volume to enjoy audios or watch videos you might want a speaker. Again you will find the Bluetooth pairing feature useful to pair a wireless speaker to your Kindle Fire so you can enjoy things at the volume that you love.

Let's Get Your Kindle Fire in the Bluetooth Pairing Mode

Step 1: Go to your home screen and access the "**Quick Actions Panel.**"

37

Amazon Kindle Fire HD 8 & 10 User Guide

Step 2: Click on the tab "**Wireless.**"

Step 3: Under the option "Wireless" you need to tap on "**Bluetooth,**" then, click on "**On**" to enable the feature.

You will know when your Kindle Fire is in the Bluetooth pairing mode by the appearing of the Bluetooth icon next to the wireless icon at the top right of your home screen.

As soon as your Kindle Fire Bluetooth is enabled it will begin to search for other gadgets that have their Bluetooth pairing mode enabled that are also compatible with your Kindle Fire.

Chapter 1: Getting To Know Your Kindle Fire HD 8 & 10

Step 4: Under the option "**Bluetooth**" select the tab "**Available Devices**" and then click the device that you would like to pair with your Kindle Fire.

The steps that will appear when you locate the device that you want to pair with your Kindle Fire are easy breezy, so, I do not need to go through them with you.

Important: *To pair your Kindle Fire with another device both gadgets must be within a certain range of each other. If you cannot locate the device that you want to pair with your Kindle Fire and you are sure that device is compatible with your Kindle Fire, then, check the range. It could be that the device is too far away from your Kindle Fire if it is not pairing while the Bluetooth feature is enabled.*

Amazon Kindle Fire HD 8 & 10 User Guide

Setting Up Your Email on Your Kindle Fire

Step 1: A lot of actions start at your home screen. Therefore, right now I need you to give your "**Home button**" a tap to navigate to your Kindle Fire home screen.

Step 2: Among the apps on your home screen please locate the tab with the "**Email Icon**" and click on it.

Step 3: To select your email provide click on the tab "**Add an Account**." A listing will be displayed with various email providers, you are now required to select the one that you use the most and want to activate on your Kindle Fire.

Chapter 1: Getting To Know Your Kindle Fire HD 8 & 10

Step 4: Your email address and password will be required. Actually as you can see there are four different fields for you to enter information.

The following information is needed in the accordingly in the fields provided:

- Your name

- Your email address

- Your password

- A description (Do not let the description field confuse you. You can enter the name of email provider that you use and that will be sufficient for the description field. Take for example that your email address is xxx@gmail.com. In the description field simply type "**Gmail.**"

Amazon Kindle Fire HD 8 & 10 User Guide

*It is time to click on the tab "**Next**" at the bottom right of your Kindle Fire screen.*

Step 5: *You already know that having shortcuts on your device get things done in less time.* Thus, synchronizing your contacts along with your email calendar dates is a definite "*Yes!*"

After the synchronizing is completed click the tab "**Save**" to move to the next step to complete the process of setting up your email on your Kindle Fire.

Step 6: Yep! Your email is now set to be viewed on your Kindle Fire and you can click on "**View Inbox**" to see the all the mails in your email account.

Chapter 1: Getting To Know Your Kindle Fire HD 8 & 10

The process to open an email is just tap on it with your and it will open for you.

Step 7: Once you open any of your emails in your inbox, you will notice three options located to the top right of your screen.

The three options are "**Delete,**""**Respond,**" and "**New**."

To remove unwanted emails tap the "**Delete**" option.

"**New**" is what you tap on when you want to pen an email from scratch. Once you click on the "**New**" tab a "**Plus sign**" will be at the top left of your screen. If you tap on the "**Plus sign**" a list of your email contacts will appear which will be the shortcut to getting the person you

Want to email information. As long as the person you want to contact email address is stored in your email it will appear on the list and you can click on it for it be added in the "**To**" field in the new email.

Tapping on the "**Respond**" option will allow a drop-down menu with three tabs to display. The names of the three tabs on the drop-down menu are: **reply**, **reply to all** and **forward**.

Important: *I discovered a great feature about your Kindle Fire and your email inbox that a lot of individuals are not aware of but luckily I am going share my discovery with you.*

When you open your email inbox on your Kindle Fire try and turn your Kindle Fire sideways. Once you turn your Kindle Fire sideways you

Chapter 1: Getting To Know Your Kindle Fire HD 8 & 10

will notice that the screen will rotate. When your Kindle Fire screen rotates it will divide the content in your inbox into two sections.

On the right of the divided interface will be the emails that you had opened and displaying to the left will be the other emails that are in your inbox.

*By looking to the top left of your screen, you will notice that there is a tab with the words "**Main Page**" please select it. Under "**Main Page**" tap on the option "**Show Folders**" to* view your "**Spam Box**," "**Starred** "and "**Deleted**" emails.

If you are wondering about adding more than one email accounts to your Kindle Fire the

Amazon Kindle Fire HD 8 & 10 User Guide

answer is a resounding "Yes," you can have more than one email accounts.

How to Add a Second Email Account to Your Kindle Fire

You can choose to go to your home screen and follow the aforementioned steps to add an email account. However, you can also add the second email account from in your email inbox.

Step 1: To add the second email account from within your email inbox, look next to the "**New**" tab there is a tab with the word "**Menu**" can you please click on it.

Step 2: Under the "**Menu**" tab you will notice the option "**Add Account**" can you please tap on it.

Chapter 1: Getting To Know Your Kindle Fire HD 8 & 10

Step 3: The same four fields that you had seen when you were adding the first email address will be displayed, kindly enter the necessary information as you had done before (in the email address field you would enter the second email address that you would like to add to your Kindle Fire).

Receiving Your Email Notifications on Your Kindle Fire

Yes, you will receive emails on your Kindle Fire by enabling the email feature but you will not be notified when the emails come.

To be notified when you receive emails you have to activate the notification feature on your Kindle Fire because is normally turned off. This feature will even allow you to decide how often you want to be notified about incoming emails.

Step 1: Tap on your "**Home button**" to access your "**Quick Actions Panel.**"

Step 2: Click on the tab "**More**" and then select the option "**Settings.**"

Step 3: Under "**Settings**" you will find the option "**Applications**" please select it.

Step 4: Kindly click on the "**Notifications Settings**" tab and then tap on "**Email.**"

Step 5: Please look to the right of the "**Email**" tab for the "**On**" button and select it.

Chapter 1: Getting To Know Your Kindle Fire HD 8 & 10

Setting a Timer for Emails on Your Kindle Fire

Step 1: All the steps that you had to follow to turn on the notification for emails, I need you to retrace that process now.

Step 2: Under the "**Email**" tab please tap on "**Contacts**."

Step 3: Under the "**Contacts**" please click on "**Calendar**."

Step 4: From the list of email addresses that you had added to your Kindle Fire kindly tap on the one that you would like receive notifications from frequently.

Step 5: Now look for the option "**Inbox Check Frequency**" and click on it.

Step 6: The time that is displayed use it to set a time for how often you would like to be notified about new emails.

Important: By selecting the "**Automatic (push)**" tab you will be notified immediately of incoming emails to your inbox.

Downloading Apps and Games on Your Kindle Fire

Step 1: Tap your home button and click on the "**Shop**" icon to the top right corner of your Kindle Fire screen.

Step 2: Look to the top right corner and please click on the "**Search**" icon, then, type the name of the game or app you want to download.

Chapter 1: Getting To Know Your Kindle Fire HD 8 & 10

Step 3: When the game or app comes in the search display click on its icon and look for the tab "**Download**" that is customarily located at the bottom right of the icon.

After you tap on the download button the game or app will start to download to your Kindle Fire.

Downloading Videos on Your Kindle Fire

Step 1: Click on your home button to go to your home screen and then look to the top of the screen for the "**Video**" tab.

Step 2: Look to right at the top of your screen for the "**Shop**" icon and then click on it.

Amazon Kindle Fire HD 8 & 10 User Guide

Step 3: Type into the "**Search**" icon the name of the video you would like to download. When the video displays in the search list please click on it and then look for the "**Download button**."

Uninstalling a App from Your Kindle Fire

*All of the prebuilt apps on your Kindle Fire **cannot be deleted.** Two of the prebuilt apps that are on your Kindle Fire are your contact and calendar.*

Any of the apps and games that you downloaded on your Kindle Fire can be uninstalled.

With that said let's get the steps of uninstalling unwanted apps and games.

Chapter 1: Getting To Know Your Kindle Fire HD 8 & 10

Step 1: Please tap your **home button** to go to your home screen and search for the app or game that you like to be removed from your Kindle Fire.

Step 2: When you locate the app or the game please use your finger to press down on it for a few seconds.

Step 3: You will notice that two tabs appear. The first tab allows you to "**Add to Favorite**" and the second tab gives you the option to "**Delete**."

Please click on the "**Delete**" tab and in a few seconds the app will be deleted from your Kindle Fire screen.

Amazon Kindle Fire HD 8 & 10 User Guide

What To Do When There Is A Pop-Up Message When Uninstalling An App Or Game?

Not all apps will give you a press and delete option. Some allow a pop-up message to appear giving you the opportunity to change your mind if you like. Let us now take a look at the process to uninstall an app or game with a pop-up message setting.

Step 1: Please just follow all the aforementioned steps to locate an app or game that you would like to remove from your Kindle Fire.

After you find the app or game use one of your fingers to press down on it for a few seconds until the two tabs appear.

Chapter 1: Getting To Know Your Kindle Fire HD 8 & 10

Step 2: I need you to click on the "**Delete**" tab. When the pop-up message appears you will be asked if you are certain you want to delete this app or game.

Click the tab "**OK**" which will be at the bottom right of your Kindle Fire screen.

Step 3: You will then be navigated to a second screen that also has a tab at the bottom of the screen with the word "**OK**" kindly click on that tab as well and your Kindle Fire will uninstall the app or game.

Features Everyone Can Use

Sometimes I get bored looking at the same color of things I use like my keyboard on my laptop for example. I wish I could change the color that it has.

I am happy to state that for my Kindle Fire that is not the case because I can change the color whenever I get bored.

You know, I am always going to share my delightful little tech treats with you and changing the color of the Kindle Fire keyboard is one such treat.

Step 1: Tap your **home button** to go to the home screen of your Kindle Fire and access the "**Quick Panel**."

Step 2: Please click on the tab "**Settings.**"

Chapter 1: Getting To Know Your Kindle Fire HD 8 & 10

Step 3: Under the "**Settings**" tab to the right you will find a tab with the words "**Keyboard and Language**" please click on it.

Step 4: Now look to the left at the bottom of the screen for the tab "**Fire Keyboard**" and click on it.

Step 5: The first option should be a tab with the words "**Keyboard Color**" please click on it.

Step 6: From the pop-up box that appears there are two options. The options are "**Dark**" or "**Light**" you can now choose your preferred color.

Important: The dark option is actually the color black and the light option the color white.

Amazon Kindle Fire HD 8 & 10 User Guide

How to Add Secondary Keys to Your Keyboard

By now you must know I love things that will let me use less time to complete my work. Adding secondary keys to your Kindle Fire is one way that you can get your typing done quicker.

Step 1: Tap on your **home button** to go to the home screen of your Kindle Fire and access the "**Quick Panel**."

Step 2: Find the tab "**Settings**" and click on it.

Step 3: Locate to the right is the tab with the words "**Keyboard and Language**" clicks on it.

Step 4: Now please look to the left at the bottom for the tab "**Fire Keyboard**" and click on it.

Chapter 1: Getting To Know Your Kindle Fire HD 8 & 10

Step 5: I need you to now click on the tab with the words "**Secondary Keys.**"

Step 7: Finally, I need you to click on the tab with the words "**Secondary Keys on All Rows**."

By the way, the secondary keys are the special characters like the ^, %, $, and so forth that you will need during some point in time when you are typing.

Why Do You Need Honey pot on Your Kindle Fire?

Over the years hackers have gotten craftier in gaining control of peoples' personal information. We too have to ensure we keep up-to-date with all the latest software to protect our devices.

Presently, **Honey pot** is dubbed one of the best protection software on the market. I am suggesting that you install this software on your Kindle Fire and so that you can be a step ahead of the hackers.

Keeping them out is your best chance of ensuring that your tech-baby is protected from their invading eyes and viruses.

You Can Have a Multi-Screen to Multi-Task

Patience is not among my strong character traits. So I like to multi-task that I do not have time to activate my impatience.

I find that using the "**Multi-Screen Multi-Tasking App**" helps me to accomplish this and you might also find it very useful.

Chapter 1: Getting To Know Your Kindle Fire HD 8 & 10

This app allows you to open more than one screen on your Kindle Fire. Let me explain things more to you. Take for example you are conducting a research about a specific topic, you can use one screen for the web browser. You will have the option to move the screen to a section of your Kindle Fire while you open another web browser or even the note pad that is prebuilt on the app.

To have more than one web browser open you will have click on the "**Globe Icon**" that is located to the left at the bottom of the. Each time you want to open a web browser when using the app just click on the **Globe Icon**. The app has a menu bar and that is where you will find the "**Note Pad.**"

Amazon Kindle Fire HD 8 & 10 User Guide

If you are a lover of music and enjoy rocking to your favorite beat while you work, then, you will find that tapping on the **music icon** on the menu bar of the app will allow you to rock to your music while conducting your various tasks.

*I am quite sure if you install this app you will find it very useful and will thank me for telling you about it. **Now let me tell you how to download the app.***

Step 1: Not to worry regardless you find that this app is very useful one of the best things about it is that is *FREE.*

At this point I need you to go to your apps store, search for "**Multi-Screen Multi-Tasking App**" and click on the download tab.

Chapter 1: Getting To Know Your Kindle Fire HD 8 & 10

Step 2: Tap on your **home button** and go to your "**Apps**" and search for the "**Multi-Screen Multi-Tasking App.**" When you find the app please click on it and go start to explore your multi-tasking app.

Chapter 2: How to Shop and Find Entertainment on Your HD Fire

If you are not a shopper, then, you must be a lover of entertainment and you definitely will want to know how to use your Kindle Fire to conduct your favorite hobby.

After all, it is all a part of the fun that comes with owning a technological device with shopping and entertainment features.

Buying and Reading Books, Magazines, and Periodicals on Your Kindle Fire

Amazon Kindle Fire HD 8 & 10 User Guide

Step 1: Click on your **home button**, then, look for the "**Books**" tab at the top of your home screen and click on it.

Step 2: Under your "**Books**" tab there are two other tabs namely "**Cloud**" and the other is "**Device**."

Important: You will find that all the books under the **Cloud tab** are the ones stored on **Amazon Cloud**. To get a book that is stored under **Cloud** to be stored on your Kindle Fire simple download the book using the "**Download Arrow**" that is located at the bottom of the book.

All the books stored under the **Device tab** are those you had downloaded and they are stored on your Kindle Fire.

Chapter 2: Shop and Find Entertainment

Step 3: Tap on the "**Shopping Icon**" to the top left of your screen and type the name of the book you would like to purchase, then, click the search icon.

Step 4: When the book is displayed that you would like to purchase click on it. Two tabs will appear. One is for you to "**Download the entire book**" and the second tab is for you to get a "**trial sample**." For the **trial sample** you will allowed to download a few pages of the book to read before finalizing the purchase for the entire book.

Assuming that you want to go ahead and click on that **trial sample** tab you will see a tab with the words "**Read Sample Now**" please click on it and the trial pages will be downloaded to your Kindle Fire immediately.

Amazon Kindle Fire HD 8 & 10 User Guide

Say you enjoy reading the **trial sample** pages and you want to complete the purchase to get the entire book, then, you will be required to click on the **back button** which will navigate you to the purchasing page. Once you are navigated back to the purchasing page you can complete your order and have the entire book downloaded to your Kindle Fire.

Nevertheless, if you did not enjoy the **trial sample**, then, you can still click on the **back button** to navigate to the purchasing page to cancel the book order.

Downloading Free Books to Your Kindle Fire

Step 1: The aforementioned steps are required to locate your **Books App – Shopping Icon – Search Icon.** The difference is this time you will

Chapter 2: Shop and Find Entertainment

type the words "**Free Books**" and Amazon free books will be listed. You can also type the word **free** before your favorite genre to search for books in that category too.

Step 2: Once you see a title that you like, you can click on it and look for the download tab. If you do not see a tab with the word download, then, click on buy and you will get the book for free.

Removing a Book from Your Kindle Fire

Removing books that you have read already and will definitely not be reading again is one of the ways that will assist you with not getting your storage used up with unwanted things.

Amazon Kindle Fire HD 8 & 10 User Guide

Important: There is one book that you are not allowed to delete because it is prebuilt on your Kindle Fire and that is the **Oxford dictionary.**

Step 1: Tap the **home button** to go to your home screen. Once at your home screen search for your "**Books**" tab at the top of your screen and click on it.

Step 2: Kindly ensure the tab "**Device**" is in the orange color and if it is not in the orange color click on it.

Step 3: Scroll through your list of books to locate the one you would like remove from your Kindle Fire. Once you locate the book use your finger to press down on it until see the follow two tabs appear:

70

Chapter 2: Shop and Find Entertainment

- Add To Favorite

 - Delete

Step 4: Please tap on the "**Delete**" tab. Within a few seconds, the book will be deleted from your Kindle Fire.

Transferring Files to Your Kindle Fire

This is the time that your USB cable will become very handy. ***The transfer process can be used to get any document, video, music or photos from your computer to your Kindle Fire.***

Step 1: Insert the smaller end of your USB cable into the cable slot on your Kindle Fire and the larger end into your computer or laptop.

Step 2: Your Kindle Fire must be on for the process to work. If the screen is locked please swipe your finger across it to unlock it.

Step 3: Once the process is being done correctly on your Kindle Fire a message will be displayed informing you that you can transfer files from your computer and a pop-up box will appear on the screen of your computer when it identifies your Kindle Fire.

Important: If you do not see the pop-up box on your computer screen take the following steps to locate it:

Click on **Start – My Computer – Kindle Fire**. When see the "**Kindle Fire Tab**" please double-click on it and your device folders will open.

Chapter 2: Shop and Find Entertainment

Step 4: Double-click on the tap with the words "**Open Folder to View Files**."

Step 5: There are two ways to select the item you want to transfer. You can either right-click on the item, then, click on cut or copy and paste it into your Kindle Fire document folder.

The second method is you can click on the item, press down on the cursor and drag it to your Kindle Fire document folder. Once you are at your Kindle Fire document folder you will release your finger from off the cursor and the item will be copied to the folder.

Downloading YouTube app on Your Kindle Fire

This is top secret information that I am about to share with you. A lot of individuals have no idea

Amazon Kindle Fire HD 8 & 10 User Guide

how to download the YouTube app on their Kindle Fire to watch free videos.

Step 1: The first part of this top secret mission is to download the free app called "**1Moble Market**" – this is a free app.

Important: This app is needed for your top secret mission because it will give you access to many other apps that are not available in the Amazon and the Android App stores.

Step 2: Go to your home screen and access the "**Quick Panel.**" Please click on the "**Settings**" tab.

Step 3: Under "**Settings´** I need you to click on the tab "**Applications.**"

Chapter 2: Shop and Find Entertainment

Step 4: I need you to now click on "**Apps from Unknown Sources**," then, tap on "**OK**" when the pop-up message appears.

Step 5: Tap the **home button** to go to your home screen. Search the top of your home screen for the tab "**Web**" and click on it.

Step 6: Now type in the words "**1Moble Market**" then click on the search icon.

Step 7: Once the page finish loading please click on the "**1Moble Market**" icon, then, scroll down the page, to right of the page you will see a tab with the words "**Scan To Download**" click on it.

Amazon Kindle Fire HD 8 & 10 User Guide

Step 8: Look to right once again and you will see a tab with the word "**Download**" please click on it.

After clicking on the **download tab** a pop-up message will appear with the question "**Download File?**" Just click on the tab "**OK**" for the file to start downloading.

Step 9: At this point you will need a file manager. Tap your **home button** on your home screen search for "**App**" and click on it.

Step 10: To the top right of your screen you will see the tab "**Store**" please click on it.

Step 11: I need you to now type the words "**File Manager Free**" in the search box, then, click the search icon and when the page loads click

Chapter 2: Shop and Find Entertainment

on the "**File Manager Free**" icon. *The official file manager is normally the second option that appears.*

Step 12: Look for the "**Download**" and give it a tap. After the app finish downloading please click on the "**Open**" tab.

Step 13: By scrolling down you will find the folder "**Download**" click on it to open it and inside you will the "**1Moble Market**."

Step 14: A question will appear asking if you want to install this application, please click on "**Next**" at the bottom right of the page.

Step 15: Now look to the bottom right of the page and click on the tab "**Install**."

Amazon Kindle Fire HD 8 & 10 User Guide

Step 16: *Hurray!* Your final two steps for the downloading of different apps are here and you will soon have the YouTube app. What I need you to do now is to go ahead and click on the tab "**Done.**"

After tapping on "**Done**" look to bottom right of your page you will see the **home page icon** please click it.

Important: The "**1Moble Market**" will be stored under "**Device**" on your Kindle Fire. So please ensure when you go to apps the tab "**Device**" is on orange.

Step 17: Go search for "**1Moble Market**" under "**Apps**" on your Kindle Fire and click on it.

Chapter 2: Shop and Find Entertainment

Step 18: In the "**1Moble Market**" app search tab please type in the word "**YouTube,**" then, click the search icon.

Step 19: Please scroll and look for the **official YouTube app**. When the page finish loading and you find the **official YouTube app** please click on it. Then look to left of the screen for the tab with the word "**Download**" and click on it.

Step 20: To know when the "**YouTube App**" finish downloading you have swipe the top of your Kindle Fire screen where you go to access the "**Quick Panel.**"

After the "**YouTube App**" is downloaded you need to click on it form the "**Quick Panel,**" then, look to the bottom right of your screen

Amazon Kindle Fire HD 8 & 10 User Guide

for the tab with the word "**Install**" and click on that tab.

Step 21: When you are prompted that the installation is completed please click on the tab with the word "**Open**" which will automatically navigate you to **YouTube**.

Important: I must inform you that if you have a **YouTube channel** you will be prohibited from login to it from your Kindle Fire. It has to do with the fact that Amazon sells videos and YouTube has them for free. I am sure you can read between the lines and understand what I am trying to tell you.

Downloading YouTube Videos on Your Kindle Fire

Chapter 2: Shop and Find Entertainment

Yes, I think I can hear you shouting praise to me for teaching you how to get YouTube on your Kindle Fire and now I am even going to demonstrate how to download YouTube videos. If I never told you before, I am going to tell you now that my guide is second to none.

Step 1: First I need you to download an app that will do more than just downloading videos from YouTube for you.

So tap on your **home button** the search for the "**Web**" tab at the top of your screen and click on it. **Step 2**: Please type in the search tab the word "**tubemate.net**" and then click on the search icon.

Step 3: You will see a tab with the words "**Download Handster**" please click on it.

Amazon Kindle Fire HD 8 & 10 User Guide

Step 4: To the left under the tab with the word "**Free**" is a tab with the word "**Download**" click on it.

Sometimes the download tab is a bit stubborn when you click on it at first. So if you do not see a pop-up message the first time you click on it, then, press down on it a little longer and then release your finger.

Step 5: The pop-up message will have a tab with the word "**Open**" please click on it.

Step 6: After you click on the tab "**Open**" the app will start downloading.

Step 7: When the app finish downloading please look to the bottom right of your screen and click on the tab "**Install**."

Chapter 2: Shop and Find Entertainment

Step 8: A bottom right of your screen you should see a tab with the word "**Open**" click on it.

You will be informed by a pop-up message how the app works and that you can start downloading YouTube videos by clicking on the "**green download button**."

It is time to test how good this app is by downloading a YouTube video.

Step 9: Tap your **home button** and go to "**Apps**" and search for **YouTube.**

Step 10: In the YouTube search bar, I need you to type the name of a video and then click on the search icon.

Amazon Kindle Fire HD 8 & 10 User Guide

Step 11: When the page loads with the video click on it to start watching it.

Step 12: I need you to look to the bottom right of the screen for the very **large green download button** and click on it.

Step 13: After tapping on the green download arrow a pop-up message will appear please click the tab with the words "**Do not show me this message again**."

Step 14: A second pop-up message will appear with the question; "**Want to download the video or continue watching**?" Just tap on **the download button**.

Bam! You can download as many videos as you like from YouTube for free.

Chapter 2: Shop and Find Entertainment

Some other cool features of tubemate.net:

Look where **the green download arrow** is at the bottom of your YouTube video screen you will see a **folder tab**.

Click on the folder to open it.

Inside are the videos that were successfully downloaded to your Kindle Fire. You have the option to change the format if you like of the videos that you had downloaded by clicking on any one of them.

When you click on any of the videos a pop-up message will appear with different options. The options that are available are: **go to YouTube**, **play as video**, **convert to MP3**, **play as music**, **save as MP3**, **delete file**, and **remove from list**.

Well that is all the information I am going to share on this awesome multi-tasking-downloading app.

Important: A good rule of thumb when you enable "**Apps from Unknown Sources**" disable it after you complete the download because if not, you will leave your device accessible for virus invasion. To disable the feature kindly go to **settings – application– turn off the Apps from Unknown Sources.**

Downloading Music on Your Kindle Fire

Step 1: Tap the **home button** and search for the "**Music app**" on your home screen. When you locate it click on it.

Chapter 2: Shop and Find Entertainment

Step 2: Look to the top right for the "**Store Tab**" and click on it.

Reminder: Anything under the **cloud tab** is stored on Amazon cloud and anything under the **device tab** is what you had actually downloaded unto your Kindle Fire.

Step 3: You will discover that music in your Kindle Music Store are divided into different categories. One such category is **album deals** which are normally the first category on the page.

The second category that you might grace your eyes on is the **new releases** and following that category would be the **recommendations from Amazon** based on your purchasing history.

Amazon Kindle Fire HD 8 & 10 User Guide

As you have noticed Amazon stocks a wide variety of music so you definitely will have to tap on the search icon and type in one of the following three options: the name of the song, the artiste name or the album name and then click search.

Step 4: Double-click on the **price button** of the item when the page loads to start the purchasing step.

If it was an album that you searched for but you only need one song from the album you will have to click on the album to view the entire song list, then, click to price button to the right of the one you actually want.

Sometimes while viewing the songs list of an album, you might see a song that you never know that the artiste sings. There is a free 30 seconds clip of the song for you to listen by clicking on the play that is located to the left of the song.

Step 5: When the purchasing step is initiated the price button will change its color to **green** and the word **buy** will be displayed on the tab. Once those two signs appear, you need to click on it to make your purchase.

Step 6: Once the purchase is completed you will be informed by a pop-up message that will also state that the song is saved in your Amazon Cloud Player.

Additionally, there are three options available. These options are: **to go to your music library**

to play, **download the song to your Kindle Fire** and **continue shopping**.

Can please click on the option to "**Go to Library**."

Step 7: You will be greeted once again with another pop-up message which will ask if you would like to automatically download your song and all future MP3 purchases that you make to your Kindle Fire?

I need you click the box beside the question in the poop-up message with the words "**Don't ask me again.**" *By selecting this option when you download music in the future it will be automatically downloaded to your Kindle Fire without this message appearing.*

Chapter 2: Shop and Find Entertainment

Then, can also please click on the tab with the word "**Yes**."

Step 8: When you want to listen your song go to the **music app** on your Kindle Fire home screen and ensure that the **device tab** is in the color orange.

Important: Songs that are stored in your Amazon Cloud can be downloaded to your Kindle Fire by going to your **music app – click on the cloud tab –press down on the song tab with your finger until a pop-up menu displays with the following tabs**:

- Add to Play List
- Shop this artiste
- Download song

Amazon Kindle Fire HD 8 & 10 User Guide

Now please click on the "**Download song**" tab and the song will automatically start downloading to your Kindle Fire.

Downloading Audiobooks on Your Kindle Fire

Step 1: Tap the **home button** and search in your "**Apps**" for the prebuilt app called**Audible.com.**

Special offers that are available to users of this app are:

-Free 30-days subscription trial

- One free credit for you to use to purchase an audiobook.

- Free daily view of the New York Times and Wall Street Journal.

Chapter 2: Shop and Find Entertainment

- A discount of 30% on your audiobooks purchase with the exception of the one that you will be using your free credit to buy.

Step 2: Tap on the **Audible.com** app and then click on the tab "**I Am New to Audible**."

Step 3: From the list provided please select your "**Country**."

Step 4: The prebuilt audiobooks in the Auduible.com app are free so you can take a listen of any one you like.

To purchase your own audiobooks tap on the **back button**, then, look to the top left of your screen for the "**Shopping Cart**" and click on it.

Amazon Kindle Fire HD 8 & 10 User Guide

Step 5: In the search box please type the name of the audiobook that you would like to purchase and then click on search icon.

Step 6: When the page loads with the audiobook click on it and then tap on the "**Buy Button**."

At this point you will be required to login to your Amazon account, follow the steps to do so and then select your preferred payment method.

Step 7: You can find the audiobook that are downloaded by login Auduible.com. You will not need to create an account on Audible.com because Amazon took care of that for you. Therefore, the same login information for your

Chapter 2: Shop and Find Entertainment

Amazon account is what you should use to login Audilble.com.

After you login Audible.com your Kindle Fire will automatically start downloading the audiobook.

Step 8: Even though the audiobook is downloaded to your Kindle Fire you will have to tap on the "**Update Button**" when you login Audible.com to see it.

Step 9: Located to the left of the audiobook there is a "**Download Arrow**" please click on it.

When the downloading of the audiobook is completed please click on it for the audio to begin.

Amazon Kindle Fire HD 8 & 10 User Guide

Located at the bottom of your screen are the pause, **play**, and **stop** buttons for the audio. A menu bar is also located to the top of your screen for you to look at the title of the chapters of your audiobook.

Bluetooth Pairing of a Speaker to Your Kindle Fire

Step 1: Tap the **home button** and access the "**Quick Panel.**" Look to the top right for the "**More tab**" and click on it.

Step 2: Please click on the "**Wireless**" tab and then click on the "**Bluetooth**" tab.

Now please click the tab with the words **on/off** enable your Bluetooth. The "**On**" must be in the color orange.

Chapter 2: Shop and Find Entertainment

I need you to please click on the tab with the word "**Searching**" that is at the bottom of your screen.

Step 3: Enable the Bluetooth feature on your speaker and then put it into the pairing mode. A light will flash on your speaker to prompt you that the Bluetooth has been enabled and is in the pairing mode.

Step 4: Look to the bottom of your Kindle Fire screen for the tab with the words "**Search for Device**" and click on it.

Step 5: The name of your speaker will show up on your Kindle Fire screen when it finds it. When the name of the speaker appears on your Kindle Fire please click on it for the paring to begin.

Amazon Kindle Fire HD 8 & 10 User Guide

As soon as the pairing is finish you will see a tab with the word "**Connected**" below the name of the speaker on your Kindle Fire screen.

Now that the speaker is connected to your Kindle Fire, you can use it to increase or lower the volume of Kindle Fire.

Mirroring Your Kindle Fire Screen to Your TV

Important: The mirroring feature will **not** work if you do not have a high definition TV. It is **not** compatible with tube TV. Your TV **must** have an HMI free input that you can insert the cable into because without the HMI input this feature will **not** work.

Chapter 2: Shop and Find Entertainment

The mirroring will only work a USB cable that has an HMI on the large end of it and a Micro-HDMI connection on the smaller end.

Step 1: The larger end of the USB cable should be inserted into the television set and the smaller end inserted into your Kindle Fire.

Step 2: Take a few steps backwards away from in front the television and you will observe that everything that is on your Kindle Fire screen is also displaying on your TV screen

Whether you want to browse the internet or watch a video using your Kindle Fire it will be displayed on your television as long as the USB cable is connected to both devices.

Happy viewing from your big screen!

Amazon Kindle Fire HD 8 & 10 User Guide

Taking Pictures with the Camera on Your Kindle Fire

Step 1: Your camera is located to the far left on your Kindle Fire home screen under the "**Photos**" tab. Once you locate it please click on it.

Step 2: To the top right you will see the "**Camera Icon**" please click on it.

Step 3: To take a picture with your camera, you will need to click the "**Camera button**" that is located to the left of the screen.

Step 4: To find the pictures you snapped with the camera look to the bottom of your screen. You can just swipe to see the all the pictures that are in your picture queue.

Chapter 2: Shop and Find Entertainment

By clicking on the "**Email**" tab you will be able send pictures from the camera app via email.

To delete a photo click on the "**Delete**" tab that is also located to the right of your camera app screen.

You can also use the "**Share**" tab send your pictures to various apps.

Step 5: If you want to find your picture folder while using the camera look below the email tab you will see an arrow. Click on that arrow to go back and it will navigate you to your picture folder.

Inside your picture folder are all the pictures you had taken with your camera and those you had also uploaded to your Kindle Fire.

Amazon Kindle Fire HD 8 & 10 User Guide

Snap with your Kindle Fire to ensure that you are storing your most treasured moments.

Chapter 3: What Really Is Alexa?

Alexa is your super-smart gadget that you can ask questions and it will definitely provide accurate answers.

Amazon has decided that they want to take the lead in producing top-notch technological gadgets and they used the Kindle Fire HD 10 to demonstrate their innovativeness by ensuring Alexa is among the features of this gadget.

When you enable Alexa your fingers will relax from hitting the keys of your Kindle Fire and your mouth will weigh in on the action to give Alexa commands.

I am about to roll out a lot of information to you that you can understand exactly how does Alexa function.

If every wanted an assistant that is tech savvy, then, made the right purchase if you own a Kindle Fire 10. The Alexa software can be thought of as your very own personal technological assistance software which is voice activated. You find that Amazon also has an Alexa App in the Amazon App store which they created as a companion for the Alexa-enabled Kindle Fire tablets.

Of all the Amazon generations Kindle Fire the Kindle Fire HD 10 is first to be equipped with the all the features of the Amazon Echo product, Alexa.

Chapter 3: What Really Is Alexa?

Enabling Alexa on your Kindle Fire 10 opens the door for you to ask limitless questions that the software will provide answers to in a jiffy. The software is not only limited to answering your questions but with the activation of its voice feature you can give it commands to perform different tasks. Take for example you want to listen music or research something on the internet using your Kindle Fire HD 10 after the Alexa feature is enabled all you have to do is tell the software to do what you want and it will.

So you have plans to go have a little fun on the road later but you are not sure what the weather will be like, then, you could ask Alexa by stating the following command: "Alexa what will the weather be like at my location at 7 p.m.?" If your Kindle Fire HD 10 screen was locked when you gave Alexa that command it will automatically lights up with a weather report being displayed on your Kindle Fire screen. You will also hear the ever polite voice system of Alexa responding to your question with the correct answer as well.

I know that might sound a bit unbelievable if you are not familiar with Alexa, but guess what, you will now have the opportunity to learn more about one the best technological personal assistant software.

Important: None of Amazon's e third and older generations Kindle Fire tablets has the Alexa feature. If you decide to download the Alexa App to install this feature on your device that is **not** equipped with the Alexa-enabled feature it still will **not** work on your Kindle Fire. Based on

Chapter 3: What Really Is Alexa?

the country you reside in some of the Alexa features might not be available.

Enabling Alexa on Your Kindle Fire

To ensure that you truly enjoy your Alexa feature Amazon even made the process to activate it fairly easy as well.

Time to be amazed!

Step 1: Your Kindle Fire must be turned on. Tap the **home button** if you are not on your Kindle Fire home screen.

Step 2: I need you to use a finger and press down on the Kindle Fire "**Home Icon**" until a blue line appears.

Amazon Kindle Fire HD 8 & 10 User Guide

Once the blue line is being displayed it acts as your indicator to inform you that Alexa is enabled and ready to be of service to you.

Some Do's and Don'ts with Alexa

Yes, it is pretty super-cool to say; "Alexa" but you actually do not have to state the feature's name each time you give it a command.

The Alexa visual that you will see on your home screen can be removed by tapping on the "**back button**" at the bottom of your Kindle Fire screen.

The fact that Alexa can be enabled, then, obviously you will need to know how to disable it as well, right?

Chapter 3: What Really Is Alexa?

Well, to disable the Alexa feature access your **Quick Panel** on your Kindle Fire home screen. Click on the tab **Settings – Device Options – click on the Alexa Icon**.

Important: The same steps you took to disable the Alexa feature can also be used to enable the feature when you want to use after it has been disabled on your Kindle Fire. However, with the **7th generation Kindle Fire HD 10** the steps to disable the Alexa feature are a little different. Here are the steps to disable the Alexa feature on a 7th generation Kindle Fire HD 10go to your **Quick Panel -Settings – click on the Alexa icon to disable or enable it**.

Now here is the thing if you are using a children's edition of the Kindle Fire Alexa is disabled by default on such tablets or if your device has an enabled parental control feature.

Once your Kindle Fire has a kid or secondary adult profile the Alexa feature will not work on your device.

If the Kindle Fire does not have 5.5.0.0 software or later Alexa hands-free mode will not work with it.

Using Alexa to Perform Different Functions On Your Kindle Fire

Activating Hands-Free Mode

Go to your home screen and access the **Quick Panel**. Click on **Settings –Alexa –Hands-Free Mode**.

Chapter 3: What Really Is Alexa?

You will have to control your Kindle Fire ESP (Echo Spatial Perception) behavior that it does not keep responding each time it comes into contact with another Echo gadget. To control your Kindle Fire ESP access the **Quick Panel** and click on **Settings** - **Alexa icon** -**Tablet ESP Behavior**.

Important: Alexa normally keep responding each time it comes into contact with another Echo device when that device uses the same wake word.

How to Use Alexa to Listen Audios on Your Kindle Fire

Audio learners and listener will be happy to use Alexa audio commands.

When you want to feel the beat of your favorite music in the soul of your heart and you want to shake your legs as you listen; giving Alexa the following voice commands on your Kindle Fire will get the job done:

- Play
- Play some music
- Play the (state the name of the song)
- Play some (be specific about the genre you would like to listen)
- Resume

Hey, do you want to adjust the volume that your music is at now?

No need to get up to do it, give Alexa the following commands:

- Volume up down

Chapter 3: What Really Is Alexa?

- Volume down

- Set volume to level (state the level or number)

Hey, that song is dope who sings it?

No, you still don't have to get up just give Alexa the following commands?

What is this?

Who is this?

What song is this?

Who is this artist?

When did this song/album come out?

Yeah, I like that song too. I would not mind listening to it again. Can you please give Alexa the following command?

- Repeat this song

You find the following commands for Alexa when you are playing music useful too:

- Show me (state a specific genre) list (this is for Echo gadgets with a screen)

Amazon Kindle Fire HD 8 & 10 User Guide

- Play me some songs I have not listen in a while

- Loop

- Next

- Pause

- Stop

- Previous

- Shuffle

- Stop Shuffle

- Next

- Previous

- Skip

- Show me my playlist

- Play brand new music

- Play this song (state a line in the song)

- Thumbs up (when you like a song when using Pandora, Amazon music, and iHeartRadio)

Chapter 3: What Really Is Alexa?

- Thumbs down (when you do not like a song when using Pandora, Amazon music, and iHeartRadio)

- Play songs from (state the specific city)

How to Use Alexa with Audiobooks on Your Kindle Fire

Important: *Alexa cannot display the text of books on your Kindle Fire screen and it cannot activate the immersion reading on your device.*

At the bottom of your Kindle Fire screen you might notice that the audio controls are still visible when you are using Alexa. You can dismiss the audio controls if you like.

Amazon Kindle Fire HD 8 & 10 User Guide

When you want to use the audio controls after you dismiss them, just access the **Quick Panel** and you will see them there.

When you want Alexa to select a title you would like to listen use the following commands:

- Play the book (state the book title)

- Read (state the book title)

- Play the audiobook (state the book title)

- Play (state the book title) from Audible

You can set a time to stop the audiobook based on how long you normally read by giving Alexa the following commands:

- Set a sleep timer for (state the specific time whether in minutes or hours)

Chapter 3: What Really Is Alexa?

- Stop reading the book in (state the specific time whether in minutes or hours)

- Cancel sleep timer

When you forget which chapter you had reached in your audiobook all you have to do is give Alexa the below command:

- Restart

Okay, you think you have an idea the chapter you had reached. Well use the following commands until you find it:

- Go to chapter (state the chapter number)

- Go back

- Go forward

- Next chapter

- Previous chapter

- Resume my book

- Pause

Yep, Alexa Commands Can Be Used With Books That Are Not Audiobooks

Important: You will have to search for books that are eligible to be used with the Alexa feature. To find books that are compatible with the Alexa feature follow these steps: **Alexa App – Menu – Music, Videos & Book. Then click Books –Kindle Fire tab.** *From the drop-down menu being displayed select the type of device you are using.*

Commands to Use with Alexa for Books:

- Play the Kindle book (state the specific name of the title)

- Pause

- Stop

- Resume

The Following Books Are Eligible to Be Used with Alexa:

- Books purchased from the Kindle Store
- Books borrowed from Kindle Owners' Lending Library
- Books borrowed from Kindle Unlimited or Prime Reading
- Books shared with you in your Family Library

The Following Books Are Not Compatible With Alexa:

- Comics
- Graphic novels
- Narration that uses speed control
- Immersion reading

If you want to use Alexa to search on the internet, shop and so forth you must activate the voice purchasing feature. To activate the voice purchasing feature take the following steps: **Alexa app- look to the left for the menu icon and click on it -Settings- Voice Purchasing**.

Important: You can only use Alexa to make purchases if you have a United States billing address and the one-click payment method on your Amazon account is enabled.

You know what would be super-coo, if you had enabled Alexa on your Kindle Fire and you give it this command right now; "Alexa, go to the next chapter."

Chapter 4: Troubleshooting and Common Issues of the Kindle Fire

I believe I can safely state that no technological device is without its own defects. Even if it takes years before the malfunction starts to frustrate you.

Likewise, the Kindle Fires come with their own set of defects. I have decided to share a few of the most common issues that customers encounter and possible solutions to those problems.

Not Connecting To Wi-Fi

Amazon Kindle Fire HD 8 & 10 User Guide

There are countless reasons this problem might exist. However, with Kindle Fires one of the main reasons it occurs is that the device is placed into the Airplane Mode.

Recently, Amazon made some changes to its device settings in regards to turning off Wi-Fi and 3G connection. With the new settings you will have to use the Airplane Mode to turn off your Wi-Fi and 3G connection on your Kindle Fire.

Once you are seeing an icon that looks like a plane on your Kindle Fire screen, then, your device is into the Airplane Mode.

Use the following steps to disable the Airplane Mode on your Kindle Fire: **Quick Panel– Menu –Settings -Airplane Mode – to the right of the**

Chapter 4: Troubleshooting and Common Issues

Airplane Mode tab click on the on/off button disable the Airplane Mode.

If Wi-Fi connection issue is not caused by the enabling of the Airplane Mode try the following methods:

- Restart your Kindle Fire.

- Please download and install the free Wi-Fi analyze app. This app can help to detect the strength of your Wi-Fi connection and you can determine if it is the cause of the problem.

- Sometimes the router is on the wrong channel and that makes it unsupported, so, check your router.

Flickering Issues with Your Kindle Fire Screen

Amazon Kindle Fire HD 8 & 10 User Guide

I put this issue on top of my frustrating encounters. Nevertheless, sometimes the solution is the very simple action of adjusting the brightness of your Kindle Fire. To adjust the brightness of the Kindle Fire, use the following steps: **Quick Panel** - **Access the notification shade at the top of the screen –Brightness - click off for the auto-brightness button**.

The second simple solution to the flickering issue is checking the cover that you had placed on the Kindle Fire. Remove the cover and see if the flickering stops.

If the above solutions do not work, then, you could contact Amazon using their Mayday feature and request a replacement Kindle Fire.

Chapter 4: Troubleshooting and Common Issues

Crashing or Freezing of the Silk Browser

When parental control is enabled on your Kindle Fire by default it blocks access to using the Silk Browser. If you believe this could be the cause of the problem, then, use the following steps to disable the parental control: **Quick Panel** - **Settings** -**Parental Controls to turn off the feature**.

A simple solution that might assist to solve your Silk Browser problem is to clear the data. Use the following steps to clear the Silk Browser Data: **Quick Panel** - **Settings– Applications – Manage All Applications** -**Silk Browser** -**Clear Data**.

When Your Kindle Fire Is Not Charging

Amazon Kindle Fire HD 8 & 10 User Guide

I told you in chapter one that using the USB cable to charge the Kindle Fire will take a longer time. So, before you start to say you have a charging issue consider what you are using to charge your Kindle Fire.

When you use the USB cable to charge your Kindle Fire by connecting to your computer or laptop it will take approximately 13 hours to charge completely.

However, using the adaptor and insert it into an electrical socket should take about 4 hours to complete the charging of your Kindle Fire

I would advise you to use the adaptor to charge your Kindle Fire.

Chapter 4: Troubleshooting and Common Issues

If you are using the adaptor, then, check if it is plugged into the electrical socket and your Kindle Fire correctly.

You can also try turning off your Kindle Fire and charge it while it is turned off.

I need you to check if your Kindle Fire has loose ports and if that is the case contact Amazon for a replacement.

What to Do when the MicroSD Card Is Not Recognized or Does Not Work

The list of Kindle Fire owners who experience this problem is very long. So do not feel alone if you are experiencing this problem. You could try the following solutions:

Amazon Kindle Fire HD 8 & 10 User Guide

One solution that might work for this issue is to charge your Kindle Fire fully. When the charging is completed for about 40 seconds use a finger to press down on the power button of your Kindle Fire. That will force your Kindle Fire to reset itself.

Second simple solution is to enable your Wi-Fi connection on your Kindle Fire and leave your device for a couple of minutes. This will give your Kindle Fire the chance to automatically download as well as install available updates on your Kindle Fire.

Third possible solution is removing the MicroSD card for a few minutes from your Kindle Fire. After the few minutes pass, you carefully replace the MicroSD card into its slot in your Kindle Fire and attempt using it.

Chapter 4: Troubleshooting and Common Issues

The fourth solution that you could try is checking the case on your Kindle Fire if you have one. Check to ensure that the case is not pressing too much against the MicroSD card.

Erratic Keyboard Typing

This is when your Kindle Fire seems to have a mind of its own that rebels against the characters you wish to type and punches its own character when you attempt to use the keyboard. Along with typing its own characters it will delete words that you type and skip pages in documents on its own.

If any of the above issues are affecting your Kindle Fire try the following solutions to see if one will work for you.

Use a piece of microfiber cloth to clean your Kindle Fire screen.

Once again the case of the Kindle Fire could be the cause of this issue so check if it is fitted properly on your device – that is if you do have a case for your Kindle Fire.

Force your Kindle Fire to power-down by holding down on the power button for approximately 20 seconds.

Important: My last possible solution for this issue is very risky. I would suggest that you only attempt this solution if you feel that you have no other choice. Please ensure that all your information is saved on a secondary storage gadget because conducting a factory

Chapter 4: Troubleshooting and Common Issues

reset will result in you losing all your information.

Here are the steps to conduct a **factory reset**: **Go to your home screen – access the Quick Panel** - **Settings – Device – Reset to Factory Default**-**Reset**.

If you took the big step of a **factory reset** and the problem still exists, then, it is time to call the bigger boss which is Amazon.

There are many other issues that Kindle Fire owners might encounter but I am unable to address all of them. I did my best to look for some of the more common issues that Kindle Fire owners have stated that they experience and suggest possible solutions.

Amazon Kindle Fire HD 8 & 10 User Guide

I do hope you can enjoy your tech-baby without any issues. However, if it does have any issues, I can only hope it is one that I have written about and one of the possible solutions that I listed can assist you.

Conclusion

Dubbed the online shopping-giant, Amazon, continuously try to produce superior products and provide satisfactory customer service.

Similar to Amazon, I am on a mission to produce superior products that will satisfy the needs of my readers. I am using the world's shopping-giant, Amazon, publishing platform to reach out to individuals around the world with the aim to help make their life more enjoyable by producing easy to read and understand guides.

I know my dream is a big one and I need your helping hands to make it become a reality. Assist me to reach more individuals and to produce more quality guides by leaving a comment. Comments help others to become aware of books and how helpful the information in the book is to others. *I look forward to reading how my guide has enhanced your Kindle Fire experience.*

It was certainly a pleasure to surf on the waves of this technological journey with you. *Enjoy your tech-baby whether it might be the Kindle Fire HD 8 or 10.*

Please leave a review on Amazon! Let others know what you think about this guide.

Thank you!

Check Out Other Books

Please go here to check out other books that might interest you:

Amazon Echo Dot: The Essential and Advanced Amazon Echo Dot User Guide for Echo Dot and Alexa by Ricardo Ward

How to Install Kodi on Amazon Fire TV Stick: Step by Step Instructions on How to Install Kodi on Your Fire Stick by Ricardo Ward

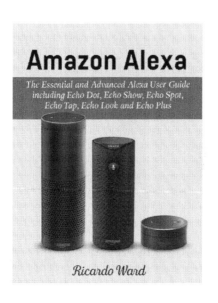

Amazon Alexa: The Essential and Advanced Alexa User Guide including Echo Dot, Echo Show, Echo Spot, Echo Tap, Echo Look and Echo Plus by Ricardo Ward

Printed in Great Britain
by Amazon